SACRED EARTH

Words for Prayer and Reflection

Cliff Reed

To Jerome and Francesca, with every blessing and thanks for all you did for the Ipswich Unitarian Meeting.

The Lindsey Press
London
2010

Published by the Lindsey Press
on behalf of The General Assembly of Unitarian and
Free Christian Churches,
Essex Hall, 1–6 Essex Street, London WC2R 3HY, UK

ISBN 978-0-85319-079-0

Designed and typeset by Garth Stewart, Oxford

Printed and bound in the United Kingdom by
Lightning Source, Milton Keynes

CONTENTS

PREFACE

Break, break, break,
On thy cold grey stones, O Sea!
And I would that my tongue could utter
The thoughts that arise in me.
Alfred, Lord Tennyson

This morning on the beach the wind roared in, ridden effortlessly by the gulls, those mournful surfers of sea and sky. Foam-crested, the mass of waters heaved with the power to sweep villages and cities to oblivion – as it has often done along this coast. The waves, exultant, crashed down on to the shingle, warning of our weakness and transience on the earth.

Moments like this remind us that something tremendous is happening around us all the time. If we are blessed, there is something within us that responds. We too are part of it. Call it by any one of countless names, but 'God' is as good as any other.

It is the outworking of the relationship between what we see of God around us and what we feel of God within us that is the life of the spirit. We express and nurture this in prayer and contemplation, in poetry and praise. And, if it is authentic, the life of the spirit will encompass every phase of human experience, no matter how painful and tragic it may be. The 'spirituality' that speaks only of peace, harmony, and happy endings is a delusion and a sham.

In this collection I offer some fruits of my own journey, in the hope that they may be useful to you in your own. Some of these reflections were written for use in worship, some are more personal, and some were written in response to events that shook the world.

Cliff Reed
Aldeburgh, Suffolk
December 2009

'I sought out Nature, never sought in vain.'
(Charles Dickens, *David Copperfield*)

SACRED EARTH

PLANET EARTH
Based on an email from astronaut Laurel Salton Clark
sent from the space shuttle 'Columbia',
31 January 2003

Earth,
our magnificent planet Earth –
lightning over the Pacific, the aurora of the south;
Africa's vast plains and America's line of life that
    joins two continents;
rivers in the high passes, Australian city glow;
the small bump of Mount Fuji, and the scars of
humanity.

So they saw it from their fragile craft,
saw moonset from among bright stars.

And can we feel their positive energy?
The energy they beamed to all of us
on our whole, shared planet as they glided by,
never to return.

May it be so.

(Laurel Salton Clark, a Unitarian Universalist from Racine,
Wisconsin, died with her six crewmates in the loss of the Columbia
on 1 February 2003.)

GREAT SOLOMON
Matthew 6: 25–34

Great Solomon,
so wise, so glorious,
is now but dust and words in a holy Book;
but the lilies still bloom
and turn their faces to the sun;
the birds still harvest
the gracious bounty of God.

We lay down our vanity
and seek the justice
of the Kingdom on this
sacred Earth.

REFLECTIONS ON WATER

Let us reflect on water:
the water we drink,
the water in which we wash our bodies and our clothes,
the water we watch: the ever-moving sea,
the tranquil sunlit pool, the deep river...

the water we swim and relax in,
the water we fish in,
the water that cools us down or warms us up...

the water that makes our crops grow,
the water that keeps all animals and plants alive;
the water of life, the living water
that cleanses and refreshes our souls
and sparkles with the life of God.

SPIRITS
John 4: 24

Are there spirits in the trees?
Are there spirits in the streams?
Are there spirits in the hills?
Are there spirits all around us,
wishing us well, wishing us ill?
Awaiting our prayers? Awaiting our offerings?
Spirits to worship? Spirits to fear?

We thought so once – but not now, not really,
though poetry and myth remember them.
Ours is a universe without spirits.

But we breathe life's breath,
and so do all the myriad creatures.
Among the crags, across the fens,
out over the heaving seas, is the
whispering, howling wind,
the breath of Earth –
the Spirit of Life.

One breath, one Spirit
in all things,
filling dust with life,
filling life with love.

'And God is spirit.'

WINGED MESSENGERS

Let us give thanks for the winged messengers.

With beauty of song and plumage,
with grace of flight and form,
they speak to us of life's everlasting miracle,
of the divine creation that never stops creating.

They speak to us of the land we live in, with
voices of forest and marshland, seashore and garden;
of hedgerow, heath, and moorland, reminding us
of the heritage that is ours to treasure and pass on.

They speak to us of lands far away, bringing
the cries of arctic wastes, the breath of
steaming jungles, searing deserts, open oceans,
reminding us that the world is one, without
borders or divisions.

We give thanks for the winged messengers
in all their variety. Let us heed the messages
with which God entrusts them.

Amen.

MAINTAINING THE FABRIC
Ecclesiasticus 38: 34

For the beauty we see around us
and for the holy ground beneath our feet;

for the heritage of faith
and for the sacred places that have come down to us;

for the loving fellowship we share
and for all who strive to make our land a better place,

we give thanks!

Together and apart, as we maintain the fabric of this world,
may our prayers be about our daily work.

SORRY FROM A TO Z
With thanks to Gary Kowalski

We mourn for the Earth and its lost creatures,
and we are sorry from A to Z –

for Atlas Bears, Arabian Ostriches, and Ascension Island Rails;
for Big-eared Hopping Mice, Bush Wrens, and Broad-faced
    Potoroos;
for Caribbean Monk Seals, Chatham Island Penguins,
    Cuban Red Macaws, and Carolina Parakeets;
for Dodos, Deepwater Ciscos, Dusky Seaside Sparrows;
    Eyle's Harriers, Elephantbirds, and Eastern Hare Wallabies;
    Four-coloured Flowerpeckers and Falkland Island Foxes;

for Great Auks, Golden Toads, and Grass Valley Speckled Dace;
   Huias, Haast's Eagles, and Honshu Wolves;
   the Ibexes of Portugal and the Pyrenees;
for Jordan's Coursers and Jamaica's Least Pauraqués;
   Koa Finches, King Island Emus, Labrador Ducks, and
   Laughing Owls;
for Mamos, Mauritius Red Hens, and Mysterious Starlings;
   New Zealand Greater Short-tailed Bats and Oahu O'os;
for Passenger Pigeons, Paradise Parrots, and Pig-footed Bandicoots;
   Quaggas and Red Sea Seals, Ratas Island Lizards, and
   Rodrigues Solitaires;
for Steller's Sea Cows, Slender Moas, and Spectacled Cormorants;
for Tarpans and Thylacines; the Tigers of Java, Bali, and the
   Caspian;
for Ula-ai-Hawanes, Cry Violets, White-winged Sandpipers, and
   White-footed Rabbit Rats; the Wrens of St. Stephen Island –
   Xenicus Lyalli.

Extinct, all of them, and many more besides, gone beyond recall
because of us, the species that leaves no room for others.
We should mourn them, along with
Yangtse River Dolphins, Yellowfin Cut-throat Trout, and
Zosterops Strenuae – the lost White-eyes of Lord Howe Island.

We are sorry, good Earth, that we have destroyed so much –
beautiful and bizarre, poetic and prosaic, famous and unknown –
and we are sorry from A to Z.

THE WAY OF AN EAGLE
A meditation on Proverbs 30: 19 and Exodus 19: 3–4
with acknowledgements to Henry David Thoreau;
Alfred, Lord Tennyson; Henry Wadsworth Longfellow; and
Conor Jameson

The way of an eagle in the sky is beyond our understanding –
it is the Maoris' child of a star;
it is the Lesser Thunderer of the Iroquois;
it is the sign of God's protection, on whose strong wings
captive Israel was borne to freedom.

The way of an eagle in the sky is beyond our understanding –
soaring in the blue empyrean as we plod wearily below;
watching from his mountain walls, a thunderbolt poised
to fall screaming and hurtling through the heavens.

The way of an eagle in the sky is beyond our understanding –
crowning glory of all wild Nature, messenger of the Divine,
calling us home to the Wilderness.

WALKING ON THE BEACH: LATE NOVEMBER
Genesis 9: 16

Walking on the beach this morning,
I saw a guillemot,
feathers clogged with oil,
vainly trying to preen and
clear away the poisonous filth.
Helpless and hopeless,
I wondered if we, who did this,
have lost our right to be here.

Walking on the beach this morning,
looking up from a glittering sea
to the rising silver sun,
I saw a fragment broken from a rainbow,
in transient fusion
with an insubstantial cloud.
Soon it faded – but maybe
the covenant endures.

HOAR FROST ON THE WOLDS
Job 38: 29

I had almost forgotten the hoar-frost –
what it's like to walk amid trees
and hedgerows so delicately dusted;
to stand by a frozen pond, its fringe
of dead reeds made beautiful with
winter's most magical adornment.
Walking these rolling hills as they sleep beneath
the gentle, freezing blanket of the fog;
finding snowdrops in the frosted wood:
I am alone with God and with
the creatures of the wild earth;
with God, 'whose womb gave birth to ice',
'the mother of the hoar frost in the skies'.

SACRED LANDSCAPES

We give thanks
for our sacred landscapes,
where God and Nature and people
all belong and are at one.

We give thanks
for our sacred landscape here in holy Suffolk,
where ancient monuments to faith
rise from tranquil valleys, bustling towns,
and rolling fields towards the eternal sky.

We give thanks today for the artists,
for Constable and Gainsborough and all the rest,
whose spirits have been stirred by our sacred landscape,
whose works bear witness to the soul's response to nature
and help us to stir our own.

O God, clear our sight to see
the beauty of our world, to
reflect it in our lives, and to
be its good stewards in the face
of all that threatens it.

FOR THE WATERS OF THE EARTH
Genesis 1: 2; Psalm 104: 25; Psalm 107: 23–24

O God, whose Spirit moved upon the face of the primeval deep;
whose works and wonders are seen by those who go down to the
    sea in ships;
whose ocean bounty is gathered with skill and hope and courage,
as it was by the first disciples;
we come before you in thanksgiving for the living waters of the
    Earth.

Grant us wisdom to care for her seas and oceans, her lakes and
    rivers,
keeping them clean and conserving the life with which you filled
    them.
Turn us from the greed and folly that leaves them dead and
    empty.

Stir within us compassion for all who make their honest living
    from the waters, risking the wrath of storm and tempest.
Teach us reverence for the myriad creatures that swim and creep
    and play there in glorious variety.

So may the waters' harvest be sustained as long as Earth shall last,
and may we share it fairly, humbly, and always with thanksgiving.
This we ask in the spirit of Jesus, for whom the waters were a
    pathway.

Amen.

IN GRATITUDE
For Beatrix Potter

God of Nature's beauty and majesty, with us
here in our gathering and in our hearts, we
remember today a woman who strove against
convention and prejudice to study the wonders
she saw around her;

who gave the world's children her timeless tales
and pictures to enchant our memories;
who farmed the fields and fells of Lakeland and
gave them in trust for the inspiration of future generations.

'Great power, silently working all things for good',*
we give thanks for the stories and the art of
Beatrix Potter, our sister in faith. Grant that we
too may leave the world richer for our living than
when we entered it.

Amen.

*Beatrix Potter's Journal, 30 September 1884

WHAT HAPPENS WHEN…?
Genesis 2: 15

What happens when the oil runs out, O God?
When we have extracted every last drop from every
dead, polluted ocean; every devastated wilderness?
When our cars and trucks stand rusting in the acid rain?
When our tractors and combines lie idle on silent farms,
when there are no petro-chemical fertilisers, no pesticides,
to flog the last blighted harvest out of the long-dead earth?

What happens when our swollen billions can no longer
depend on the plundered riches of the garden Earth,
which you entrusted to our care?

Of course, we know the answer,
if we only had the humility to see it.
But you won't save us from our own stupidity, even if you could.
You've warned us often enough, shown us the way of wisdom –
but we scorned it.

So, what happens when the glaciers melt and the rivers run dry?
When the forests are deserts and the seas have risen in revolt?
When war and meltdown have laid waste our cities?

If there is hope, it lies within us,
but time is running out.

Maybe it already has.

Miserere.

DIVINE UNITY

Out of the Divine Unity we came.
In the Divine Unity we live and move
and have our being.
To the Divine Unity we will return.

There are no beginnings and no endings,
save those we impose to cope with eternity.
There is no knowledge of the Great Mystery,
save the precious fragments we are given
in recompense for our strivings.

For what we receive we give thanks,
and turn our faces to the light.

May it be so.

THE EARTH ENDURES
Iken Church, Suffolk – Lent

The Earth endures, O God,
but we do not,
so who are we to save it?
We are but dust and ashes.

Grant us wisdom
to be your good stewards;
so may the Earth sustain us
while your breath is in us.

Amen.

COMMUNITY IN INFINITY

If there is an infinity of galaxies in the universe;
and if there is an infinity of stars in each galaxy;

and if only an infinitesimal percentage of those stars
    have planets orbiting round them;
and if only an infinitesimal percentage of those planets
    have evolved life;

and if only an infinitesimal percentage of those living planets
    have evolved intelligent life;
and if only an infinitesimal percentage of that intelligent life
    has developed advanced civilisations –

then there are countless millions of planets in the universe
    that sustain advanced civilisations.

But since these advanced civilisations are impossibly remote
from each other, it is unlikely that any of us will ever meet.
And yet we are all out there.
And we are one, as all we
who live on Earth are one.

SACRED EARTH

GATHERING FOR WORSHIP

THE BELOVED COMMUNITY
Letter to Philemon, verse 16

We gather to uphold the liberty of the human spirit
and to reject all that would enslave it.

We gather to be the beloved community where no one
is a slave, and everyone is a sister or a brother.

We gather to uphold the truth that makes us free
and the Divine Unity that makes us one.

BUBBLES
With apologies to Gautama Siddartha

Bubbles in the river we may seem to some –
transient, insubstantial, empty;
but we are here to effervesce with loving worship,
to reflect the divine rainbow in our fragile souls,
to treasure within us, for a moment, the breath of life.
Yes, it matters that we are here – together!

WELCOME
With thanks to the Revd. John Fairfax (1623–1700)

Welcome to this house of prayer,
'where we meet not only one with another,
but all with God'.
Through the generations we have come
to celebrate the love that is divine,
to be its human channels to each other,
and to reflect the light of hope on to
the world's darkness.

DRAW NEAR
Letter to the Hebrews 10: 19–20, 22, 24

This is a holy place –
enter by the true and living Way,
draw near with true hearts
to consider one another
and the works of love.

SPIRIT AND EARTH
Based on words in the Gospel of Philip

From the Spirit and the virgin earth we come,
called to heal the wounds of separation.

Male and female we come, made one and
equal in loving community.

In worship and in fellowship we come,
to glimpse the trees of Paradise
and catch the fragrance of their fruits.

THE TREASURE WITHIN

May we keep the flame of truth
burning brightly among us, and by
its light find the treasure within
that is courage, wisdom, and loving kindness.

HERITAGE OF LIGHT

We light our chalice
to celebrate our heritage of light:
the light of science and of art;
the light of story and of poem;
the light of nature and of reason;
the inner light of spirit and of truth.

CHILDREN OF ABRAHAM

We are all children of Abraham,
whether we be Jew, Christian, or Muslim.
In our worship we seek the One God
of our kindred faiths – and the reconciling
spirit of peace, justice, and mutual respect.

THE LIBERAL LIGHT

We kindle the light of our liberal faith: may it be
the light of knowledge to dispel ignorance,
the light of reason to dispel superstition,
the light of love to dispel bigotry and inhumanity,
no matter what their guise.

THIS LIGHT

We kindle this light to be for us
the light of God that shone in Jesus;
the light of hope that shines in every human soul;
the light of truth that guides each loving, free, and
    open mind.

SACRED FIRE

We kindle the sacred fire
as we gather in community,
mindful of the brave souls and
questing, independent minds
whose courage won our freedom.

IN THE DARKNESS OF GRIEF

In the world's grief and darkness
we keep a flame burning –
the flame of hope, the flame of truth,
the flame that warms the heart with loving kindness.

ANOTHER LIGHT

We kindle our chalice flame.
By its light we meet each other
face to face.
In each other's faces
may we sense another light,
the one divine Light
that glows within us all.

A LIGHT IN DARK PLACES
With acknowledgements to J. R. R. Tolkien

We kindle our chalice flame.
May it stand for the inner light
that is given us – to be a light in dark places,
a light when all other lights go out.

THE WAY

We light this chalice
to bring light to our minds,
wisdom to our souls, and
warmth to our hearts:
light to show us the Way,
wisdom to walk it truly,
warmth to enfold our fellow
pilgrims with compassion.

TO FIRE

Source of light
bringer of warmth
burn gently
burn gently in our midst
burn gently

HOUSE OF THE SPIRIT'S FIRE
With acknowledgements to J. R .R. Tolkien

This is the flame of the Spirit
and this is the house of the Spirit's fire.

We come to sing our songs
and tell our tales.

We come to be quiet,
wishing for peace and thought,

For this is the house of the Spirit's fire.

FLAME OF THE SPIRIT (I)

Flame of the Spirit,
blazing in the wind of Pentecost.
Flame of the martyrs' witness,
blowing in the gales of history.
Flame of the liberal faith,
rising from the crescent Earth
to celebrate our blue planet and its web of life.

Chalice of humanity,
calling all to share God's grace
and bounty with justice and equality.
Chalice of the common cup,
welcoming without condition
all who come to worship in goodwill.
Chalice of our world community,
from which we drink the wine of love
to make us one in freedom.

FLAME OF THE SPIRIT (II)
For John Biddle (1615–1662)

Flame of the Spirit,
kindled in our hearts
and in our worship,
come among us
as God's minister
to make us holy.

SACRED EARTH

BLESSINGS

THE COMING DAYS

God of our hearts,
bless us as we part.
Be with us as we face
the quandaries, fears, and puzzles
of the coming days.
Send your peace among us,
and through all our troubled world.

Amen.

GREAT POWER
Based on words by Beatrix Potter

'Great power, silently working all things for good',
surround us, infuse us, and sustain us
as we leave this sacred place to walk the earth,
our common home.

Amen.

WE LEAVE THIS HOUSE

We leave this house
with the blessing of the Spirit we have shared.
As we go out to walk the green Earth
under the vault of heaven,
we remain one body,
whether together or apart.

Amen.

THE COMMON CUP

We gathered as the family of God.
We have drunk from the common cup
of our heritage, tradition, and faith.
Now we go out as witnesses of
Divine love and human fellowship
to our one, yet fractured, world.

May it be so.

ONE SPIRIT

Spirit of the earth,
bless us.
Spirit of the waters,
bless us.
Spirit of fire and the burning sun,
bless us.
Spirit of the air,
bless us.
With the blessing of the One Spirit,
may we go in peace.

DREAMS AND VISIONS

Come to us in our dreams, O God;
grant us visions of our world at peace with itself
and give us the determination to make them real.
Send us out from here with love and courage in our hearts.

Amen.

SPIRIT OF PROPHECY
Luke 1: 51–53

Spirit of prophecy,
who spoke in Mary
of filling the hungry,
humbling the proud,
and casting down the mighty,
be with us as we part.
Curb our own arrogance,
open our hearts to human need,
and make us strong for
those who need our strength.

Amen.

AFFIRMATION

ON BEING RELIGIOUS LIBERALLY

To be religious
is to be open to transcendence,
closing off no possibilities
in our dullness and our pride.

To be religious
is to connect our own deepest intimacy
with the universe's unimaginable ultimacy.

To be religious
is to connect with each other in compassion,
trust, and justice; always loyal to what we
know is true and right and good.

To be religious
is to move beyond our small denials that we may
worship, giving our spirits wing to rise in joy.

To be religious
is to recognise the shadow and include it, lest
too much light should blind us to another's pain.

To be religious
is to be humble before the Mystery – within us,
around us, and among us – raising hands in praise,
joining hands in love.

Let us be religious, bound together in freedom.
May it be so!

THE SPIRIT DANCES ON

The Spirit dances on
through galaxies and stardust,
from the moment of creation
to the moment these words are spoken.

The Spirit dances on
through evolution's life story,
filling all that lives and all
that has ever lived –

the distant ancestors whose genes are ours now;
the hopeful monsters whose lines
were written out so long ago,
while the Spirit danced on.

The Spirit dances on,
giving life to our feeble bodies,
making them dance too, burning them out,
for they cannot dance for long.

The Spirit dances on,
and we do too, our de-incarnated spirits
caught up once more into the One Spirit,
returning whence they came, dancing on
to who knows where.

The Spirit dances on,
and so do we – for ever.

THE CHRISTIANS WHO MOVE ON

We are the Christians who move on,
leaving behind what cannot be retained:
the creeds written to cement a long dead empire;
the justification for slavery, genocide, and witch-burning;
the refusal to hear another's truth;
an idolised book, a man diminished to a god.

We leave these behind and move on,
not in arrogance, not unaware of tradition's worth,
not creating new bigotries as bad as the old ones,
or so we hope!

We move on,
carrying with us the free and timeless heart of Jesus,
faithful to what was said and done, in love, for liberty –
by him, by those who follow him, by those who give
his spirit voice and flesh in every time and place.

We are the Christians who move on,
leaving even the name behind, maybe,
a name that Jesus never knew.

We are the Christians who move on,
seeking and sharing the divine heart
in every one, as Jesus did.

MEDITATION FOR CENSUS DAY
Based on questions in the 2001 UK National Census

What is your name?
   My name is what I have left when
      every other possession is stripped away.
What is your country of birth?
   The world is my country.
What is your ethnic group?
   All ethnicities are mine, for I am human,
      and humanity is one.
What is your religion?
   I am *Christian*, because I try to follow
      God's rule of love, as Jesus did.
   I am *Buddhist*, because I reverence the Buddha's
      way of compassion for all beings.
   I am *Hindu*, because I see the Divine Unity
      in a myriad avatars.
   I am *Jewish*, because the Law still guides me
      and the Prophets still challenge me.
   I am *Muslim*, because I bow before the One God,
      the beneficent, the merciful.
   I am *Sikh*, because I heed the Gurus' witness to
      the worth and oneness of us all.
   I am of *other religions* too, for the truth has
      many channels, the divine so many messengers.
   I am *Unitarian*, because I embrace the unity
      that I see in all.

Count me as a child of your universe, O God.
So be it.

THE UNIVERSAL CONSCIENCE

Whatever our quality of faith concerning God,
whatever name we use to praise the Ultimate,
whatever sacred way we claim to take,
whatever sage or prophet we invoke,
whatever avatar or epiphany we say commands our heart,
it will suffice – if we act rightly according to love and conscience.
At the last, may their testimony witness to a life
that healed and blessed the world as best it could.
And in that may we be granted peace.

PRAYER

IN AN UNQUIET WORLD

God of our hearts,
whose Oneness makes us one,
in an unquiet world, let us be quiet.

In an unpeaceful world, let us be peace;
in an unkind world, let us be kind;
in an unjust world, let us be just;
in an unloving world, let us be love.

Make of our speaking the things you want us to say;
make of our deeds the things you want us to do;
make of us what the world needs us to be.

So may our lives be a blessing to all,
and our spirits the channels of your Spirit.

May it be so.

FOR A DISTRICT MEETING

As we meet together in these springtime days,
gathered from our diverse fellowships and
congregations, we ask a blessing on our meeting.
May your Spirit be among us, O God.
Help us to deliberate and decide with love in our
hearts and wisdom in our minds, ready always to
listen and willing to speak when we need to.
We ask this in the spirit of Jesus and all your messengers.

FOR A MEETING

God of our hearts, Spirit within,
be among us now,
connecting where we feel no connection,
stirring us to the love we find so hard.
We meet in your name, and
in the name of noble values
and high principles.
Help us to be true to them,
for too often we are not.
Help us to know, recognise, and
admit our failures – the times
when we have judged unfairly,
the times when we have hurt
instead of healed.
Help us to be big enough to be sorry,
to take the path of reconciliation when
pride and obstinacy have driven us apart.
Help us to rise above our pain
and recognise each other's.

We meet to serve you and your people,
not our own vanities and conceits.
God of our hearts, Spirit in our deepest selves,
guide us and connect us.
This we ask in the name of
all your messengers.

Amen.

GOOD SHEPHERD
Ezekiel 34: 12
(with a quotation from 'The sheep', in 'The Fairy Caravan',
 by Beatrix Potter)

Good Shepherd,
we thank you for your loving care,
for your guidance that keeps us from falling,
for your strong hands that rescue us,
for your compassion that seeks us out when we are lost.

We are wanderers in the wilderness of the world.
We are not as surefooted as we like to think.
We don't know the hidden pits and precipices
that are around us on every side.

You are the Good Shepherd,
seeking out your scattered flock in the cloudy and dark day.
Teach us to care for each other and to hear you
'calling, with a voice like a bell, across the frozen snow'.

WE THIRST
John 4: 6–15

Thirsty, we come to drink at Jacob's well.

We drink and drink, but we will thirst again.
We have a thirst its waters cannot slake.

We thirst for that which makes us whole,
turning our desert souls into verdant pastures.

IN THE SOCINIAN SPIRIT
(inspired by the preface to the 1665 edition of the Racovian Catechism)

God of truth and loving kindness, we gather in your
name, as so many have done before us, to seek and
speak the truth in love and comradeship.

Save us, we pray, from the arrogance of telling others
what they should believe. Give us courage and clarity
humbly to witness to our own faith without harming
or oppressing others.

We ask that each and every person be free to express
their heartfelt beliefs and honest questionings, and that
they allow other people the liberty to do the same.

And though we claim the right to advance our own
thoughts in matters of faith and the spirit, help us
never to wrong others or attack them as we do so.

This we ask in the Spirit that fills all your true servants.

Amen.

SPIRIT OF LIGHT AND DARKNESS

'The Lestrygonians and the Cyclops,
the fierce Poseidon you will never encounter,
if you do not carry them within your soul'
(Constantine P. Cavafy, 'Ithaca')

As we gather on this bright morning,
we may forget the darkness in which
our fears take hold; the subconscious
caverns where dwell the things that
trouble our dreams and sometimes
fill our nights with monstrous terrors.

At times they even break into our
waking hours, robbing us of peace
and confidence, casting shadows
over the light of day. At the root
of our being, something gnaws away
at our faith, our hope, even our love.

Spirit, who dwells in the darkness and
the light, grant us courage. Help us to
understand the hidden things we fear.
Remind us that when we face our mythic
beasts, our demons and our dragons, the
monsters of the id that haunt our inner
shadows, you are there with us and we
need not be afraid.

May it be so.

LIGHTEN OUR STEPS

God of our hearts,
lighten our steps as we walk upon the earth.
Help us to read your book of life in the lilies
of the field, as Jesus did.

Teach us new ways to live,
that our cities may be safe and beautiful;
our countryside bountiful and green to
nourish our bodies and our souls.

In the tragedies and disasters we blame on nature,
show us how often it is our folly and injustice that
cause them or make them worse.

Give us the wisdom and compassion for which
our struggling world hungers and thirsts. Remind
us that we *all* need them – not just our rulers and
other people, but each one of us.

God of our hearts,
enlighten our spirits as we walk upon the earth.
We ask this in the name of all who have made
your Spirit theirs.

Amen.

PEOPLE OF THE BOOK

'People of the Book, let us rally to a common proposition, to be binding both on us and on you, that we shall worship only God...'
(Qur'an, 3: 64)

One God, proclaimed by all true prophets and messengers,
we bow before you in prayer.

Grant us the wisdom to know you as Oneness, the Divine Unity,
embracing all the names with which we address you –
all humble and reverent worshippers, all humanity, all life,
and all Creation.

We give thanks for the revelation of your will and nature
in the sacred books that are but one Book.

With gratitude we recognise your revelation in the natural world
and in the human heart; in all works of love and beauty
that flow from you.

We are grateful for the justice that your laws inspire, and for the
compassion and mercy with which we should administer them.

We give thanks for all men and women whose kindness, courage,
and benevolence bless the world with your loving Spirit.

We grieve and we are ashamed that some have taken your Book,
torn out the pages, cut up the chapters, shredded the sentences,
then used the fragments to turn us against each other.

We are People of the Book that you have written in all tongues
and on hearts made ready; help us to unite in what we share and
to forbear in what we don't.

May it be so.

PRAYER TO THE DIVINE UNITY

O Thou,
whose Oneness includes and embraces
all that has been made and has come to be;

O Thou,
in whom all things are present and
who is present in all things;

O Thou,
in whom there is no division, a Divine Unity,
and whose expression in humanity found focus
and symbol in Jesus, our brother;

help us to know what it is to be God's child,
and so be fit vessels of your universal presence.

PATERNOSTER IN BRIEF

Loving God of many holy names,
rule in our hearts and on the earth
which feeds us. Forgive us as we forgive.
Test us gently and protect us.
This we pray, as Jesus did.

Amen.

FOR OURSELVES

We pause to be conscious of that which
makes each of us unique –

the colour of our eyes and hair and skin;
our height and build; the face that is ours
alone; the inner self that no one knows;

our heritage of genes and family, of culture
and of faith, with which we build
our own special lives;

the abilities and disabilities that give us our
potential to grow and create as no one else can;

the place where we live – the town or city,
the village, coast, or countryside – that helps
to make us who we are;

our interests and hobbies; our taste in music,
books, or fashion; our likes and dislikes – all
the things that make us distinct.

Let us give thanks for who we are:
as individuals, each one unique;
as humankind, in which our individuality
contributes to the whole.

Let us respect and celebrate our own uniqueness,
and each other's too.

May it be so.

FOR OUR COMMUNITY OF CHURCHES

Divine Unity, fount of life and love,
we pray today for our community of churches.

We pray for the congregations which form
its membership, and for all who maintain their
worship and witness.

We pray for the willing volunteers who serve at
local, district, national, and international levels.

We pray for our denomination's dedicated staff,
conscious of the burdens we lay upon them
and the thanks we fail to give.

We pray for all who devote their lives to ministry,
giving thanks for their vocation and their service.

We pray too for those layfolk who serve as pastors
and leaders in our communities of faith.

In times of uncertainty and change, we pray that faith
and wisdom be strengthened,
and restored where they are lost.

Grant us the power of love to heal all division,
and may faithfulness to you be the bedrock
of our fellowship.

This we ask in the spirit of Jesus, our brother.

Amen.

WISE AS SERPENTS
Matthew 10: 6, Luke 23: 24

God of our hearts,
in an imperfect world
may we go out as
sheep among wolves;
as wise as serpents
and as innocent as doves.

Help us to be trusting
but not gullible,
open-hearted
but not empty-headed,
ready to think the best
but prepared for the worst.

May we never become hardened
against the humanity of others,
especially those who are
themselves the victims of deceit
and exploitation; those who
never learned the better way.

Help us to be kind, even as we
stand firm against the human
instruments of malice and evil,
remembering always the prayer
of Jesus: 'Forgive them, for they
know not what they do.'

THE CIRCLING YEAR

FOR THE NEW YEAR

We gather on this first Sunday of the year
to renew our flame of love and fellowship
in hope of better days to come for us
and everyone on Earth.

JOURNEYING IN HOPE
'Welcome from God, O glad New Year! Thy paths all yet untrod'
(John White Chadwick)

God of our inmost hearts, we turn to you
at the start of another year.

No one knows what it will bring, and we
make our plans in hope, not certainty.

As we set out once more on the journey, we pray
for courage and guidance in the way of love.

Help us to hold to the truth we know, and to
resist the lies and follies that beguile the world.

Open our eyes to see the needs of others,
Our ears to hear your call in their unhappiness and discontent.

Make us listen to the Earth and what she has to teach,
for the sake of all your children.

In humility we turn to you, O God. Help us to
make this year a better one than anyone dared hope!

We ask this in the spirit of Jesus, and of all your messengers.

Amen.

EPIPHANY

We remember, O God, the coming of the Magi to
Bethlehem; the story of three fabled kings bearing
gifts that spoke of glory and suffering to come.

Help us to see in them the working of your will
for us today.

From distant lands they come, telling us that
Jesus came for all the peoples of the world,
not just his own.

From different times they come – kings of
past, present, and future.

They say that you came to us in all holy,
brave, and loving souls of the years that
are gone; that you come to us today with
comfort and challenge in our turbulent,
unpeaceful world; that you will always
come, as long as humankind endures.

They travelled through lands of fear and
treachery, of brutality, sorrow, and despair.
And yet they held to the star of hope and
trusted to your guidance.

Our world, our lives, our lands know
evil and darkness. Grant us a Magi's faith and
endurance to find the way through.

continued overleaf

They came to a child's crib, the story says,
and paid homage to the divine hope it cradled.
May we too see you and hear you in the innocent
and the helpless – and love you there.

Amen.

A COMMUNITY OF LOVE AND RESISTANCE
A chalice- or candle-lighting for Holocaust Memorial Day
27th January

This flame calls us to worship, fellowship,
    and loving communion.
It calls us to the celebration of all that is kind and good and true.
And this flame calls us to resist the inhuman,
    to challenge malice and untruth,
and to stand for the right, no matter what the cost.

FOR HOLOCAUST MEMORIAL DAY
27th January

We stand in solemn silence and remember
the names that stand for genocide –

Auschwitz, Sobibor, Majdanek;
Dachau, Buchenwald, Bergen-Belsen;
the list goes on and on...

Tasmania, Wounded Knee, Armenia;
Halabja, Bosnia, Rwanda;
the list goes on and on...

The names of places where humanity
failed to be human.
The names of places where we
reached the depths.

We stand in solemn silence.
We hear the words of the Kaddish
spoken in memory of the millions dead,
each one an individual, a murdered person.

We honour them as lost kin.
We honour those who resisted evil.
We honour the righteous of the nations.
Would that we had been among them.

GOD OF THE LONELY PLACES
Lenten Prayers at Iken Church, Suffolk

I.
In the peace and beauty
of this sacred place,
this wilderness of water and of sky,
be with me,
Spirit of God,
to guide,
to comfort,
and to strengthen
against all temptations.

Amen.

continued overleaf

II.
O God of the lonely places,
whose Spirit drove Jesus
into the wilderness, and
brought me here today
to this church of the
river and the winds,
be with all who seek
your presence in the
solitude.

Amen.

LENTEN PATERNOSTER
A responsive prayer

Our Father,
  who art in heaven,
and our brother, your son, who walked
the earth and died for love,
  hallowed be thy name,
and his, in every tongue.
  Thy will be done,
though we find it hard to do, and to bear,
  on earth,
our Mother, in her beauty and her pain,
  as it is in heaven,
the infinity of space and spirit.
  Give us this day our daily bread,
to break in fellowship as Jesus broke it,
  and forgive us our trespasses,
against you, against him, against each other,
and our better selves,
  as we forgive those who trespass against us,

if only we did!
and lead us not into temptation,
for we are weak and may fail the test,
but deliver us from evil,
which is born and grows in our wounded souls,
for thine is the kingdom,
which always awaits us,
the power and the glory,
revealed at Easter,
for ever and ever,
while the universe lasts.

Amen.

MOTHERING SUNDAY
A chalice-lighting

May the warmth of our chalice-flame be to us
a reminder of the warmth we knew
in our mother's womb,
a promise of the warmth we seek in this
community of the way of love.

A MOTHER'S LOVE
'We feel the happiness of true creation when we give birth to a child.
The beat of a mother's heart is wonderful music: bearing the
reassurance of dawn, the warmth of noon, the purple of sunset.
It is, in one word, wholeness.'
(Kinga-Reka Szekely, Unitarian minister and mother in Transylvania)

We come to give thanks for the mothers who bore us
and nurtured us; to celebrate the love and kindness
we received from them.

continued overleaf

We come to give thanks for the children entrusted
to us for a little while. Holy One,
be with us in both the joy and the grief they bring.

We come to give thanks for this wonderful creation,
for our Mother the Earth, and for the glory of life
in which we share.

FOR MOTHERS IN SLAVERY

On this Mothering Sunday
we give thanks for our mothers;
for the life they gave us, and for
the love with which they set us
on life's road.

We remember, too, the mothers
who bore their children in slavery,
who had their children torn from
them to be sold. We give thanks
for all who strove against this evil.

And remind us, Spirit of Liberty,
that slavery still blights our world.

As we celebrate nature's miracles,
make us conscious of the women
who are still trafficked and enslaved.
Be with them, O God, in their
degradation and their fear.

We hold them in loving thought
and pray that women everywhere –
mothers, sisters, daughters –
be delivered from slavery and
oppression of every kind.

And we pray for the strength to
play our part in making it so.

Amen.

THIS DAY OF HOPE
A responsive prayer for Palm Sunday

On this day of hope we remember, O God, the ride of
your servant, Jesus. Sharing his spirit we come into
your loving presence.
   May all your names be hallowed.

He rode against the evils and corruptions that invade
our souls. With him we seek a better way to be human.
   May your Rule come among us.

We would, like him, live according to your love,
citizens now of the Kingdom he proclaimed.
   May your will be done on earth.

We acknowledge our dependence on your Creation and
repent the arrogance with which we have blighted it.
   Give us this day our daily bread.

continued overleaf

We haven't loved you as you would have us love.
We haven't set aside our prejudices and selfishness.
Forgive us the wrong we have done.

Cleanse us of all bitterness and resentment.
Open our hearts to the way of reconciliation.
We forgive those who have wronged us.

We know our weakness. To follow Jesus on Palm Sunday
is easy, but what if we must follow him to
Gethsemane and Calvary?
Do not bring us to the test.

The world's people yearn for peace and healing.
We pledge ourselves to that cause.
Save us from evil.

We take our stand with Jesus and with all who do
your will in every age and faith. Not for our glory
but for your saving truth – or so we pray.
*For yours is the Kingdom
and the power and the glory
for ever.*

Amen.

HOLY WEEK: A BLESSING

From raised hopes to disillusion;
from fellowship to betrayal;
from gentle triumph to brutal death;
this is the drama of Holy Week.

May we pass through it in full awareness
of its timeless truths, learning compassion
and courage, trusting always that after
darkness comes the dawn. Go in peace.

ETERNAL MARTYR
For Good Friday

We remember, today, the eternal martyr:
who offends the bigotry of others
and threatens their selfish insecurity;
who is the repressed conscience
and the uncomfortable truth –
integrity amidst corruption.

He is crucified, she is shot;
he is gassed, she is burned;
he is poisoned, she is hanged;
she is raped and beaten, he is tortured and broken.

You are with your martyr, O God,
in the pain and anguish,
giving courage and strength;
the peace of death and the
triumph of the spirit's resurrection.

We give thanks for the eternal martyr
and what was bought with his death, her blood.
But we confess our part in his murder and her torment.
And should we be called to martyrdom, help us to
be worthy of our calling.

May it be so.

'WHAT IS TRUTH?'
John 18: 38

'What is truth?' asked Pilate, as if he cared.
The truth was Rome and her power, that's
all that he, or anyone else, needed to know.

Against her, not even the whole Jewish nation
had stood for long. Why should he care what
this crazy mystic said? The 'king' of some other
world than this! As if there was one!

Rome's empire is but a memory now.
The crazy mystic's kingdom was not
of Pilate's world, the world of history
and power politics and earthly might.

The crazy mystic's kingdom is not of
this world either, the world of history
in the making, of power politics and earthly
might, where war's first casualty is truth.

What is truth? Not the lying propaganda of
a tyrant. Not the well-spun briefings of generals
and politicians. Not the rumours, exaggerations,
and loaded half-truths of the story-hungry media.

The truth is death and suffering, fear and pain.
The kingdom is in the love that heals and comforts,
frees and reconciles. The crazy mystic's kingdom is
in this world, but not of it; ruling in human hearts.

That is all the truth we need.

IN THE BREAKING OF BREAD
An Easter meditation on Luke 24: 32 & 35;
scripture quotations from William Tyndale's
translation of the New Testament (1534)

'Did not our hearts burn within us while he talked with us by the
way, and opened to us the scriptures?'

When did the fire of revelation last burn within us?
When did we last hear Jesus speak to us?
Or let him?

How often do we open the Scriptures?
Or open our minds to them?

Spirit of resurrection and rebirth, walk with us
on life's road; reveal to us its wonders, duties,
and purposes.

'And they told what things were done in the way,
and how they knew him in the breaking of bread.'

We have walked with Jesus so many times
but have not known him.
In many guises he has explained the truth to us,
but we have been too dull to see it.

May we, in loving communion and shared fellowship,
know him at last in the breaking of bread.

BREAKFAST ON THE BEACH

'He comes to us as one unknown.' – Albert Schweitzer
Easter meditation on John 21: 1-13

Breakfast on the beach.
Fresh fish sizzle over a charcoal fire.
New loaves, warm from the oven, lie in a basket.
The beckoning aromas mingle in the still, morning air,
wafting over the lake where pied kingfishers dive and
a fishing boat heads for shore.

'Come and have breakfast!' – an invitation from a
stranger, from one unknown; an invitation to
restored community, to shared pleasures,
and good company after hard work.

Where, now, is Jesus –
carpenter, cook, and friend of fishermen?

Not in a distant heaven, not in books of doctrine,
not in philosopher's creeds:
Jesus is where people gather to share in warm
and wholesome fellowship.

God of our hearts, help us to know you
in the richness of your Creation.
Bless all who care for it, so that its bounty
may never end.
May we know you in the stranger
who invites us to share it lovingly,
generously, and wisely.

Amen.

SPRINGTIME BLESSING

May the blessings of the earth delight our springtime days,
and may the love of God that flowered in Jesus
be with us, in us, and between us, for ever.

Amen.

SPIRIT OF UNBOUNDED LIFE

In the glory and beauty of springtime
we turn to you in humble gratitude,
O Spirit of unbounded life.

Our hearts leap as the skylark sings
in the heavens, and all around us is
blossom and bursting, freshest green.

We rejoice, and bow our heads in wonder.

But, for too many, the season's joy
and beauty is dimmed by fear –
fear of unemployment and poverty,
fear of homelessness and bankruptcy,
fear of a future without hope.

Spirit of unbounded hope,
come to all who dwell in fear's shadow.
And come to us, that our community of
faith may help to lift the gloom, reflecting
in our worship and our fellowship, in our
words and our deeds, the ancient promise
that 'All shall be well'.

continued overleaf

In love for all who despair this day, we
pledge ourselves to be your messengers
of better days to come.

May it be so.

HOLY SPIRIT: FOR WHITSUNDAY

Holy Spirit, Breath of God,
that came to prophet and apostle,
come to us, we pray.

Pour down upon us
as life-giving rain;
make our souls bloom
like the desert.

Rest upon us
as tongues of fire,
kindling our souls
to be beacons of hope.

Come to us as guide,
leading us into all truth,
as Jesus promised.

Come to us as comforter,
raising us when we fall
crushed by an unforgiving world.

Come to us as advocate,
witnessing to love's endurance
when doubts oppress.

Holy Spirit,
touch us with your liberty;
give us the right words to speak.

Make our spirits one with you,
our very selves the vessels of
your being.

FATHERS' DAY CHALICE LIGHTING

We light this chalice
to celebrate the light
that shines in each of us –
women and men,
adults and children.

And on this Fathers' Day
we light it for all those
who have known the
joys and quandaries
and griefs of fatherhood.

HYMN FOR HIGH SUMMER   (8.7.8.7.)

When the turtle doves are purring
in the hedgerow and the copse,
and a gentle breeze is playing
over fields and green tree-tops;

When the white clouds in the blue sky
cast cool shadows on the earth,
and the meadow grass is stirring,
swaying to the Spirit's breath;

continued overleaf

When, above, the swifts are wheeling
and, below, the wise ants toil,
garnering the bounteous harvest
of the sun- and rain-drenched soil:

Souls are touched and, for a moment,
even sorrow's burden lifts;
we give thanks for all these blessings,
all the summer's countless gifts.

INVOCATION FOR HARVEST

Placed here by God and evolution,
we give thanks for this garden-planet;
pledging to till it with wisdom
and to care for it with humility.
For this we gather, for this we worship.

HARVEST THANKSGIVING

At this celebration of harvest we give thanks
for the golden grain we saw in our summer fields,
and for its harvesting.

We give thanks for the fruit of our orchards and vineyards,
for the vegetables that swell in the rich earth
or grow green in the sunshine and the rain.

We are so blessed, and yet we take it all for granted.
Forgive us.

We hold in our loving thought and prayer the people
of our one world who suffer the devastation
of natural – and not-so-natural – disaster.

We pray for the lands where the harvest seems one
of hatred and of death; where terrorism, cruelty, and
war raise bitter crops of misery and vengeance.

We give thanks for the harvests of earth and spirit.
We pray that all who are denied them now will
soon receive their bounty through the workings of
your love in human hearts like ours.

This we ask in the spirit of Jesus
and all your messengers.

Amen.

IN THE FALL
*With acknowledgements to J. M. W. Turner
and 'The Fighting Temeraire'*

Now autumn comes,
and the year is a great ship
on its way to the breaker's yard,
its transient glories
fading in the fall.

But the transient
is also the eternal and will come again.
Lead us on, Great Spirit, to new life,
new glories, and the time of resurrection.

DACHAU
On the sixtieth anniversary of the martyrdom of Norbert Čapek,
12 October 2002

How can we
who stand here
on this grey October day
know what they went through?

How can we
return to our lives
so smoothly, so easily,
when they could not return to theirs?

How can we
take our humanity
for granted
when humanity died here?

WE WEAR RED POPPIES
For Remembrance Day

We wear red poppies.

Once, in the beginning, they were white;
but their roots reached down
into the stinking mud
and drank the blood
of generations slain,
turning their petals red.

And that is why we wear red poppies.
There is no going back.
Miserere.

FOR HUMAN RIGHTS DAY
10th December

God of our hearts, Spirit of liberty,
we remember and celebrate today
those who began and those who continue
to define and establish the human rights
of all men and women:

those who resist the crushing weight of
persecution, slavery, and oppression;

those who dedicate their lives
to the relief of suffering, to defying tyranny,
and freeing the unjustly imprisoned;

those who speak and write and preach against
the denial of human worth and dignity;

those whose struggle is moved by love and compassion,
not hatred and the thirst for vengeance.

Remind us that rights have matching responsibilities;
that we cannot claim for ourselves the rights
that we deny to others.

God of our hearts, you are there wherever the human
triumphs over the inhuman and so becomes divine.
To this you call us. Strengthen us to respond.

Amen.

ADVENT: HOPE OF ANGELS

The light of Christmas beckons
and we stumble towards it once again,
through doubt, distraction, and despair.

Be with us on the journey, we pray,
Spirit of him who came and is to come;
give us hope enough to hear the angels,
and to help others hear them too.

Amen.

AWAITING CONJUNCTION

As we kindle our Advent flame,
the shepherds on their dark hillside, somewhere
out of time, are undisturbed by angels.
In their fabled palaces, the Magi have yet to see
the new star and wonder what it means.
Myth and history await conjunction.
The timeless tale awaits re-telling,
and hearts await its promise of a new beginning.

WINTER LIGHTS

We light our chalice candle
to greet the winter solstice
and shed its glow on the
hinge of the year.

We kindle our chalice light
as Jews kindle the lights of
Chanucah. May they burn for
freedom and the rights of conscience.

We kindle our chalice flame
to welcome Christmas – almost come –
'King of the Seasons all!'

AS CHRIST DRAWS NEAR

We light our light
to bring alight
the longest, darkest night
of all the year.

We light our light
to lift with light
the thickest, deepest gloom
from all who fear.

We light our light
to greet with light
the brightest, holiest star
as Christ draws near.

THE GREETINGS OF CHRISTMAS

The greetings of Christmas are about merriment,
happiness, and joy – and so they should be! It is
the season of love's hope renewed; the tilting of
the earth towards spring.

But there is grief at Christmas too, there always was,
and loneliness and suffering: three sorrowing guests,
and we must give them room.

We celebrate Christ's coming, remembering those
for whom he came, God's gift of light: the dwellers
in darkness and the shadow of death.

May our love enfold them too, and may we all be
guided into the way of peace.

THIS CHRISTMAS

This Christmas I give thanks once more for the birth of Jesus,
for his message of the rule of love, and for the ultimate integrity
with which he lived it.

This Christmas I give thanks for all the great souls who have
turned our world towards the light, and for the bright festivals
that remember them.

This Christmas I give thanks for all the blessings in my life and
for the love that has enfolded and inspired me from my own birth
to this present moment.

This Christmas I give thanks for my family: those present in fond and sacred memory; those still around me, laying down new memories for our lives' enrichment.

This Christmas I give thanks for friends both close and distant (however that be understood!) and for all who share with me the path of life and faith.

This Christmas I give thanks for the past year, touched as it was by both grief and joy; by the silence of death's shadow, and by the song's of life's celebration.

This Christmas I give thanks for this glorious universe; for the divine in nature and moments of insight and rapture; for the companionship of all who share the breath of life.

This Christmas I feel shame for our weakness, unkindness, and stupidity; for our failure to care for each other and for the Earth; but I give thanks that sometimes we care enough to be ashamed.

This Christmas I give thanks that, in our caring, God calls us to continue the struggle for love and truth and righteousness, and gives us the heart to do so.

This Christmas I give thanks for you, my fellow pilgrims. And I wish you and all the earth the blessings of healing, peace, and restoration.

Amen.

SAINT STEPHEN'S DAY: FOR THE WORKERS
26th December
'When a poor man came in sight, gathering winter fuel'
(John Mason Neale)

Let us give thanks for those who, gladly and willingly,
doggedly and determinedly, do the work that we would
find it hard to do ourselves:

work that is too dirty and dangerous and unpleasant
for us to contemplate;

work that would test us beyond the limits of our
capabilities, be they physical, mental, or emotional;

work done at times when we would rather be at rest;
in places we would rather not go;

work that would pose too great a challenge to our
tender consciences, though it must be done;

work with people we would rather not have to meet
or think about;

work that might just cost us our lives, as it may cost
the lives of those who do it now.

For all these workers we give thanks, O God, for on
them we depend. Be with them in their labours;
help us to appreciate them as you do.

Amen.

SAINT JOHN'S DAY: FOR THE WORDSMITHS
27th December
'And the Word was made flesh and dwelt among us...'
John 1: 14

Divine Word, who speaks in us for our re-creation
and salvation, we give thanks for the wordsmiths
whom your gift of words has inspired:

for those who reveal to us the secrets and strivings
of their souls, that we might better understand and
nurture our own;

for the poets whose words move, delight, and challenge us,
weaving webs in which are captured wonder, joy, and pain;

for the storytellers, bards, and skalds; the novelists,
playwrights, and scriptwriters, who transport us to
other worlds that we might better understand our own;

for those who bring to us the arcane mysteries of
science in words that we can comprehend, and help us
in our striving to understand the universe;

for those who bring us news from our tumultuous world,
the information with which to make
our choices and our judgements;

for those whose skill is to translate the words
of others, reversing the Babel curse and restoring
the wholeness that was lost.

Divine Word, made flesh that we might hear,
we give thanks for all the honest, healing wordsmiths
of the world.

Amen.

HOLY INNOCENTS' DAY: CHILDERMASS

28th December
'Watch where he comes walking
Out of the Christmas flame.
Dancing, double talking:
Herod is his name.'
(From 'Innocent's Song', by Charles Causley)

Herod and his goons stand cursed eternally,
along with all the murderers of innocents in every age.
For the unrepentant there is no way back.
The cherubim stand guard with a flaming sword.

The curse lies too on the murderers of innocence:
who take young minds and fill them with hatred;
who corrupt young souls with false, inhuman values;
who rob them of childhood's love and bliss and wonder.

These murderers wear many guises. Their faces may be fair,
their voices sweet. But it would be better for them
to be drowned in the sea with millstones round their necks
than to face the judgement that awaits them.

SAINT THOMAS BECKET'S DAY: THE MARTYR

29th December
'For wherever a saint has dwelt, wherever a martyr has
given his blood for the blood of Christ, there is holy ground,
and the sanctity shall not depart from it.'
(From 'Murder in the Cathedral', by T. S. Eliot)

A heavy door slams open
and mailed footfalls echo
in the sacred gloom.

Harsh cries, protests
brushed aside – and
a man at prayer.

The swish of cloaks
thrown back, the ring
of swords unsheathed.

The crunch of steel on bone;
a kneeling figure falls, and
then a momentary silence.

Four swordsmen, knights
of the king, sweep out
of the cathedral.

Behind them, on the cold
stone, are the body, blood,
and spilled brains of Becket.

So a martyr saint was made,
who valued God's service above
his life, his monarch, and his friend.

On a cold night at Christmas
holy blissful Thomas paid the price that
each of us may, one day, have to pay.

Miserere.

REMEMBERING THE MAGIC

'It's she that makes it always winter. Always winter and never Christmas; think of that!'
(From 'The Lion, the Witch and the Wardrobe' by C. S. Lewis)

It is the sixth day of Christmas
and the snow has come, warming
my heart with its cold and gentle beauty.

Adults don't like the snow.
It's inconvenient and messy and stops all those car journeys
that, mostly, they don't really need to make.

Children love the snow.
They thrill to the magic that remakes
the world with short-lived purity.

And I love the snow too!
I always have and I always will.
I know I shouldn't. I'm much too old. But I do.

When it comes to snow,
the boy I was stirs in me and longs to be
whistling down a hillside on a swift toboggan.

That boy read a book about an enchanted land
where it was always winter but never Christmas.
He didn't know how true this is of many human hearts.

I cannot look out now on lamp-lit snow
and not be in that enchanted land of childhood,
where Christmas came at last to break a tyrant's spell.

The child dares to believe that
by the Spirit's power of love and liberty
all ruthless tyrants should be toppled from their thrones;

that God's warm breath can thaw the frosty heart,
give courage to the weary and the weak, bring back
to life the hearts long turned to stone.

I know that grown-ups don't believe such foolish things.
That's why the magic has departed from their lives; and
why they cannot enter kingdoms where the Christ-child reigns.

NEW YEAR'S EVE: THE DYING IN THE NIGHT

'Ring out, wild bells, to the wild sky,
  The flying cloud, the frosty light:
The year is dying in the night.'
(Alfred, Lord Tennyson)

Another year of God is dying in the night.
We pause to offer thanks for all it gave
of love and joy and faithful living, all it
brought of wisdom and compassion.

Many lives have passed into the Great Mystery
during this dying year. Many went too early,
some went when they should, and some were
overdue. For all who mourn, we ask consolation.

Despite all grief and evil, this year saw much that
was good, much to celebrate, much that was done
for human welfare. For the achievements, the new
lives, and all revelations of Divine Love,
we give thanks.

Amen.

FOR THE LAST DAYS OF CHRISTMAS

'The road from Bethlehem dwindles in twisted tinsel...'
(Francis C. Anderson)

Tree lights still twinkle
in front-room windows,
but this Christmas is fading
and the New Year brightens
imperceptibly.

May the spirit of the season
outlast its trappings
and, like the Magi,
may we travel into
the unknown future
by the light
of the Christ-child.

This we ask in his name
and those of all your messengers.

Amen.

ANOTHER YEAR OF GOD

'Another year of life's delight;
Another year of God!'
(John White Chadwick)

Another Christmas draws to its close;
the spirits of the Magi pass by once again
on the road to Bethlehem.

Together we enter another year of God.
May we face it without fear, a community of
the free and living Spirit.

REFLECTION

WHERE IS YOUR GOD?
'"Where is your God?" they say...'
(James Martineau)

My God is in the swirling majesty of galaxies, and in
the fundamental components of whatever matter is,
both light and dark.

My God is in the breath of every life that breathes
the atmosphere of Earth, and of every kindred
planet there must be.

My God is in the wisdom of the ages, and in every
truth discovered by the human mind and heart.

My God is in the voices of the prophets,
the witness of the scriptures, the sacrifice of martyrs.

My God is in the human spirit, moving it to
kindness, steeling it with courage, healing it
with love – as Jesus showed us.

My God is in the thirst for justice that is denied
to others, and in the impulse to mercy when it
is denied to us.

My God is in the beauty of Creation and in its terrors too,
calling us to reverence and compassion.

My God is in the communities we make,
helping us transcend our fearful selves
to know the Oneness that is Divine.

IN THE BEGINNING

Ecclesiastes 11: 5, 7–8
'The close similarity between man and the lower animals in
embryonic development ... cannot be disputed.'
(Charles Darwin, 'The Descent of Man')

In the beginning
a speck of life, miraculously charged,
growing, changing:
now it grows gills like a fish,
now it is like an amphibian,
now it could be a young lizard,
growing, changing;
then it is clearly a mammal,
something like a rabbit, maybe,
or will it be something like a dog?
Or will it be something else?
A tail comes, then goes, as it grows
and changes in the warm darkness.

At last, through nine months of evolution,
it has become a child, ready to be born.
And so a woman comes to have within
her womb a living body and a human spirit,
the work of the Maker of all things.

The light of our days is sweet, O God,
and however many there may be,
help us to rejoice in all of them.

Amen.

MORNING STAR

Meditation on words by the Venerable Bede
in 'Apocalypsum', II, 28

'Christ is the Morning Star
who when the night of this
world is past brings to his saints
the promise of the Light of Life
and opens Everlasting Day.'

Let us not question these words.
Let us not pick and quibble.
Let us not fail to catch the power
of their faith and to respect it.

Let us be touched by their beauty,
moved by their assurance.
Let us imagine the comfort they brought
when life was fragile beyond our imagining,
flickering weakly in a dark age.

But life is still fragile
in our troubled world.
Our age is as dark as any other.

Divine Spirit, who fills the Morning Star with
the Light of Life, give us words of hope and faith
to bring to our darkness and the world's.

STAR MAKER

Meditation on words from 'The Machine Stops', by E. M. Forster

Star Maker,
whom once we tried to make in our own image,
believing ourselves the noblest of all creatures visible,
we pause in stillness.

Century after century
we have woven garments for ourselves,
garments of thought and ingenuity,
shot through with the colours of culture,
sewn with threads of self-denial.

Once they seemed heavenly –
when we wore them loosely
and could shed them at will.
But they have stiffened and tightened
and strangled us with our own arrogance
and illusion.

Could we shed them still?
Rediscover the naked divine essence
of body and soul – and live by it?
Rekindle the colour of our tired, faded ideas?
Can our spirits grasp again the stars
from which we came?

Star Maker,
teach us the humility that makes us free.

NO ABIDING CITY

'For here we have no abiding city...'
Hebrews 13: 14

Let us reflect on the fragility of the city,
the skin-deep nature of civilisation.

The world is full of lost, deserted cities.
Once they bustled with commerce;
their temples and churches echoed
with the voices of priests and peoples,
witnessed rituals of blood, rituals of
beauty that raised the soul to heaven.

Those cities lie drowned beneath the waves
or choked with desert sands;
they are grass-grown hummocks
or jungle-cloaked ruins.
Nature destroyed some, reclaiming her own.
People destroyed others.
On earth there is no abiding city.

Civilisation is as frail as the city,
engulfed by the waters of chaos
as the levees fail. Only that law
endures which is written on the
human heart. For that we pray,
O Spirit of the Ages.

THE SON OF GOD PASSED BY TODAY

The Son of God
passed by today
on his way to the pub,
but no one noticed.

They were all
on their way
to church –
for once.

In one church
they ate the
Son of God –
or thought they did.

In another church
they shouted his name a lot
but seemed more interested
in turning themselves on.

In another church
they doubted whether there was a Son of God,
or whether there was a God either,
for that matter.

But the Son of God
just let them
get on with it,
as he always has.

And down the pub
he talked with
a broken friend
and brought him back to life.

THE WAY, THE TRUTH, AND THE LIFE
Meditation on John 14: 6

'*I am the way*', says Jesus –
   for I am the path for you to follow,
   the walk of love for you to walk,
   the lighted track to guide your footsteps
   to God's presence.

'*I am the truth*', says Jesus –
   for God shines in my humanity, and can in yours;
   with my voice he speaks, and can with yours;
   in the memory of me he draws you close.

'*I am the life*', says Jesus –
   for in me God's breath was a mighty wind and
   a gentle murmur; in me a new humanity was born.

'*No one comes to the father except by me*', says Jesus –
   but not just as one man long ago,
   nor as a god, for I was never that.

I am every human soul who submits to God.
I am the one gate keeper who is all the prophets,
messengers, and great souls of our kind.
I am the door to the one house with many rooms.

One God of all who turn to you
in spirit and in truth, help us to know that,
in our differences, we too are one.

PICTURES AT AN EXHIBITION
*Meditation on John Goto's 'Loss of Face', 104 images
photographed in churches in Norfolk, Suffolk, and Devon*

Medieval piety created them –
to adorn the barrier to the holy of holies,
the screen that bore the rood and shielded
the sacred rite: pictures to exalt excluded souls
and feast their eyes with hallowed imagery.

Faces of saints and kings, wimpled women and
bearded prophets, looking out with sad reflection
as the generations pass; the radiant angel inviting
to salvation; grinning Death to warn that time is short.
So they remained unchallenged through the centuries.

Then Puritan piety defaced them,
driven by the Second Commandment to rid God's house
of graven images and purge the church of
Satan's wiles. And so men came to gouge the
downcast eyes and gash the mouths that spoke
a heretic prayer.

They came in righteous indignation
to hack and scour until their fury was appeased.
And now, across so many centuries the faces
still look out, where eyes remain, through the scratchings,
through the scrapings that sometimes
seem like hands raised vainly to defend.

They look into a world they never dreamed of,
neither they nor their destroyers.

Continued overleaf

O God, once served by image makers and image breakers, help us to honour all true piety and never think we have the right to judge another heart that truly loves you.

Amen.

WAR AND PEACE

WAR AND PEACE

We would turn our backs on war,
but not on the victims of oppression.
We would opt for peace,
but not forget our duty to the weak.

We would seek the peaceful path,
but not if it leads us into self-righteousness.
We would try to love our enemy,
but without betraying our neighbour.

We would cry, 'Peace, peace',
but never suppose that crying is enough.

Let us sacrifice our consciences
rather than sacrifice the helpless.
Let us see that war has no glory,
but easy peace no virtue.

Let us hold to the Divine Way,
knowing it can lead through darkness.
Let us turn our backs on war,
but know that sometimes we must face it.

O merciful and compassionate One, in our doubt
and our perplexity guide us in the right path.

IT IS EASY TO CRY 'PEACE'

It is easy to cry 'peace'
when we are not oppressed by tyranny.
It is easy to invoke patience
when our loved ones are not in chains.

It is easy to call for restraint
when our children are free from fear.
It is easy to be even-handed
when your sister is not being raped
and your brother is not being tortured.

It is easy to mouth smooth pieties
when cruelty and injustice are not before your eyes.
It is easy to quibble about legalities
when you have laws that protect you.

It is easy to debate rights and liberties
when terrorists haven't strewn your streets
with bloody, broken bodies.

It is easy to light candles
when your family isn't burning,
or to sing sweet songs when hatred
isn't screaming in your ears.

It is easy to be sure
when we are far away,
safe in our certainties.

Spirit of Love, don't let us use you
to excuse our failure to relieve those
who suffer torment at human hands,
or to make a difference when we can.

FOR THE VICTIMS OF TERROR

'We laid it down that whoever killed a human being,
except as punishment for murder or other wicked crimes,
should be looked upon as though he had killed all mankind.'
(Qur'an, sura 5, verse 31)

God of love,
merciful and compassionate One,
we hold in our thoughts today
the innocent victims of terrorism,
and all who suffer violence, cruelty,
and inhumanity at human hands.

In particular, we think of those
we name now in our hearts...

Send them your Spirit of
comfort, strength, and courage.
Bring them an awareness of
your loving solidarity.

And in our own sense of
helplessness and desperation,
save us from misdirecting our
anger and blaming those who
are not to blame.

Amen.

HELL – AS SEEN ON TV

I switched on the TV today
and saw yet another country
that no-one's ever heard of
wracked by hatred and violence;
with too many people on too little land,
sunk in misery and poverty
with little prospect of escape.
What little peace there is –
and there is precious little –
is kept, as usual, by hapless soldiers
from disunited nations far away.
The programme finished
and I moved on, but that
god-forsaken country did not.
Lord, have mercy upon us!

CHALICE OF PEACE

Out of the fires of war
let us kindle the chalice of peace.
Out of the fury of battle
let us create a passion for peace.
Out of the turmoil of conscience
let us weave the calm of peace.
In the one Spirit that we share
let us celebrate the vision of a
world made just and free – and
find the strength to build it,
a little at a time.

SACRED EARTH

PASSAGE

FOR BLESSING A MARRIAGE

God of love,
whom Jesus taught us to know as father,
we ask your blessing on *N* and *N*
as they stand before you, joined
in the free and affectionate bond
of marriage.

We thank you for the gift of loving
commitment that has grown between them;
and we thank you for the love and care with
which they are to build a family. May it be
rooted in the grace of mutual understanding
and true respect.

Guide and strengthen them in ever-deepening
devotion to each other, and in selfless devotion
to all whom you entrust to their care. And make
of their home a place where your love shines in
theirs; a place of blessing to all who live
and come there.

We ask this in the name and spirit of Jesus,
your son, our brother.

Amen.

FOR THE SICK

We pray for the sick, the injured, and the wounded –
   may healing be theirs, and relief from pain.

We pray for those who love them –
   who sit by hospital beds or wait anxiously
   at home, knowing no peace.

We pray for all who care for them –
   called to heal, to nurse, to ease the path to life
   renewed, or perhaps to death's release.

We pray for all of these –
   thinking especially of those who are known and
   dear to us as we name them in our hearts...

   Amen.

NO EASY THING
For the funeral of a young man

It is no easy thing to celebrate a life
when all we feel is emptiness.
It is no easy thing to be grateful when
all we feel is bitterness and anger
at the injustice of it all.
It is no easy thing to be joyful when our
hearts are overwhelmed with grief.

But let's remember his face. Let's remember
his smile, his laugh, his love, his friendship.
Let's think what he would want us to do.

Continued overleaf

So although our hearts are broken and our
tears flow, let's go deeper – to the founts
of love, finding there the strength to give thanks
that he was part of our lives, and
always will be.

Amen.

IN MEMORY

We gather as a community of faith.
It is the autumn of the year, a time of
dying and of loss. We are conscious
today of someone who was often with
us here, but has now passed from us.

We give thanks for her life and all that
she brought to our worship and fellowship.
We miss her unique personality, so much
a part of the church we form by coming here.

We thank you, O God, for her time with us.
We thank you for her friendship and her love;
for all the kindness and happiness she brought
to so many down the years.

May peace and rest be hers,
and ours when the time comes.
We ask this in the spirit of Jesus.

Amen.

STILL LISTENING

Around four o'clock
I catch myself still listening
for keys in the door,
for the calls of boys
come home from school.

But no keys turn,
no boys call,
for they are boys no longer
and their lives are elsewhere.

And there are those
who listen for keys
that can never turn again,
for calls that can never come –
and shall they be comforted?
I pray that it might be so.

INDEX

Lightning Source UK Ltd.
Milton Keynes UK
UKOW03f0619160813

215445UK00001B/109/P